Abigail Adams

A Adams

by Liz Ray

HOUGHTON MIFFLIN HARCOURT
School Publishers

PHOTOGRAPHY CREDITS: **Cover** © CORBIS. **Title page** © The Granger Collection, New York. **2** © American School/ Bridgeman Art Library/Getty Images. **3** © The Granger Collection, New York. **9** © The Granger Collection, New York. **11** © The Granger Collection, New York. **14** © The Granger Collection, New York. **16** © The Granger Collection, New York. **17** © CORBIS.

Printed in China

ISBN-13: 978-0-547-01663-4
ISBN-10: 0-547-01663-8

6 7 8 9 0940 18 17 16 15 14 13
4500396626

Trouble Brewing

Boston was a tense place to live in 1770. Colonists were angry about having to pay taxes to the British king. They were tired of obeying laws that they did not help make. Red-coated British soldiers, called "redcoats" or "lobsterbacks," patrolled the streets, reminding the colonists that Britain ruled over them.

Abigail Adams was one of the colonists who lived in Boston. Her husband, John Adams, was an instrumental leader who would become the second President of the United States. Abigail could often hear soldiers' feet marching loudly outside her windows as the troops drilled in the nearby square. Despite the tensions, she enjoyed the lively city, visiting friends and caring for her home and family. But on the night of March 5, 1770, Abigail heard much more than marching feet outside her window.

A map of colonial Boston

A crowd of angry colonists had gathered. They were mocking a British soldier. When the soldier hit a man, the crowd began to throw things. More British reinforcements were called to control the mob. The peal of church bells rang out, which usually summoned all able-bodied townsmen to fight a fire. But in this case, the fight was against the British.

John Adams was the lawyer who defended the British soldiers when they went on trial for the Boston Massacre. Although he wanted American independence, he believed that everyone had the right to a fair trial.

Through the window, Abigail could hear shouts and screams as the soldiers fired their muskets into the crowd. More troops rushed toward the center of town. When the smoke cleared, three colonists were dead. Two others would also die from their wounds.

The crowd dispersed, but the soldiers remained, lining the streets in a show of force. Abigail worried that this incident, soon to be called the "Boston Massacre," would lead to more violence—perhaps even war. She had no idea that this incident marked the beginning of major changes in her own life.

Like most women of her time, Abigail had grown up expecting that she would devote herself to her husband and children. Her mother had taught her to clean a house, cook, sew, grow vegetables, raise chickens, and take care of the sick. At that time, girls were taught only the basics of reading, writing, and simple arithmetic at home. They were not sent to school as boys were. However, Abigail's father had a large library, and he encouraged Abigail and her sisters to read literature, history, poetry, and books about politics. Abigail was determined to educate herself. She grew up to become one of the best-read women of her time.

Abigail's thirst for knowledge led her to take an interest in the politics of the day. She and her husband spent many hours discussing the growing resistance to British rule. So when John came home a few months after the Boston Massacre to tell her that he had been elected to the Massachusetts Assembly, Abigail understood what that meant. The Massachusetts Assembly was one of the first groups of colonial legislators who wanted independence from England. John's new position meant that he would be gone from home even more. He would also have less time to make money to support the family. Worse yet, as a member of the Assembly, he could be labeled a traitor by Britain. This would put not only him but also Abigail and the children in grave danger.

Abigail burst into tears when he told her of his election. Yet she bravely agreed that he should serve. She told him that she was willing to share in the danger and difficulties that would come.

Not Just Women's Work

Over the next few years, John's duties often took him away from home. Abigail and her four children returned to their small farm in rural Braintree, about 10 miles from Boston.

Even when John was home, Abigail worked hard on the farm. She cooked all the family's meals in the fireplace, using heavy iron pots and pans. She made their clothes, tended the garden, and took care of the livestock. They had cows for milk, sheep for wool and meat, and chickens for meat and eggs. They also owned horses to plow the fields and for transportation. Abigail grew all the vegetables, including onions, potatoes, and pumpkins, that they would eat during the winter when the garden was covered with snow. Abigail also took care of their four children, teaching them to do chores, read, and behave properly. She was busy from dawn to dusk!

But when John was elected to the Continental Congress and left for Philadelphia 300 miles away, Abigail's life became even harder. She knew she would have to be very efficient to do her own work and John's, too.

Abigail was now in charge of hiring and firing farm workers. She had to get mud, sand, and seaweed to fertilize the fields. She had to make decisions about planting and harvesting and organize the mowing of hay to feed the animals. Abigail was also personally in charge of all the family finances and supervising the tenants who rented farmland from John. She even had to make decisions about John's law practice while he was away! She worried about war and missed her husband. Some wives might have resented their situation. Yet Abigail felt that this was her way of helping the cause of American liberty.

Abigail worried about her new responsibilities. She wrote long letters to John, seeking advice on tasks she was unfamiliar with. But it could take two weeks for her letter to reach John and another two weeks to hear back from him. This didn't stop Abigail from doing what had to be done. She made many decisions on her own and gradually grew more confident in her ability to run the farm by herself.

"I hope in time to have the Reputation of being as good a *Farmeress* as my partner has of being a good Statesman."

— *Abigail Adams*

Abigail's letters were important to John. Not only did she write about their family and farm, she also described political events in and around Boston. Abigail's interest in politics and her powers of observation provided John with vital information that he could not get elsewhere. John sometimes showed her letters to other members of Congress and even quoted from one during a speech.

"[A] Lady at the Foot of Pen[n]'s Hill...obliges me... with clearer and fuller Intelligence, than I can get from a whole Committee of Gentlemen."

— John Adams

Abigail's Writing Being self-taught, Abigail's handwriting was not as good as that of more educated people. This bothered Abigail because good handwriting was thought to mark an educated person. Abigail's spelling and punctuation were also not what she would have liked. When one of her sons teased her about this, Abigail declared that she always tried to make her meaning so obvious her readers would know what she meant. Self-conscious about her own writing skills, Abigail had a strong desire to see good education available to women and girls.

War!

On April 18, 1775, Paul Revere made his famous ride to warn colonists that British soldiers were marching to Concord. American minutemen and British troops engaged in battle. The war for independence had begun!

When she heard the news, Abigail didn't panic. In fact, she felt calmer than she had in a while. She had been expecting fighting to begin and was ready for it. Besides, Concord was 20 miles away—quite a distance in those days. Although John's brother invited her and the children to move in with him, Abigail bravely decided to stay on the farm as long as she could.

Even though there was no fighting nearby, Abigail's life was turned upside down. People fleeing the British in Boston needed places to sleep, and Abigail opened her home to many of them. Some people stayed only a night, while others lived there for a week or more. When Continental soldiers on their way to Boston stopped to rest, Abigail fed them and gave them something to drink. One time, a whole company of colonial soldiers spent the night. Some stayed in the attic, while others slept with the animals in the barn. When they practiced their drills behind the house, Abigail's eight-year-old son Johnny proudly mimicked the marching right alongside the soldiers! Abigail described the house to John as "a Scene of Confusion… you can hardly imagine how we live."

Early on the morning of June 17, 1775, Abigail woke to the thundering sound of cannons. Outside, she saw smoke from the guns in the distance. She and Johnny climbed Penn's Hill for a better view of the battle.

Townspeople watched the Battle of Bunker Hill from afar.

The Americans were defending two hills overlooking Boston—Breed's Hill and Bunker Hill. As British soldiers stormed Breed's Hill, the Americans obeyed the order, "Don't fire until you see the whites of their eyes." Firing from too far away was a waste of ammunition. The Americans ran out of ammunition anyway, and the British captured the hill.

Abigail didn't know any of that at the time. All she knew was that cannons boomed all that day, through the night, and well into the next afternoon. The sound of guns upset everyone so much that even the most routine household tasks became impossible. She wrote to John, "The constant roar of the Cannon is so distressing that we cannot Eat, Drink, or Sleep." When she finally did get news of the battle, it was not good. Hundreds of soldiers had died. A dear friend of theirs, Joseph Warren, was among those who had been killed.

During this time, John continued to write to Abigail. He described the progress Congress was making. Abigail liked getting the letters, but she was growing increasingly unhappy. John's absence and the harsh conditions weighed on Abigail. In one of her letters, she asked John, "Does every Member [of Congress] feel for us? Can they realize what we suffer?" She described the hardships the people of Boston faced. She said that they were forced to stay in their homes and often had no fresh vegetables or fish.

Abigail did what she could to help those who suffered. She continued to let those who had lost their homes stay in her house, or she helped them find other places to live. Abigail heard that one of John's friends needed a place for his family to stay. John owned several houses that he rented to tenant farmers. A man named Hayden lived in one of these houses. He hadn't paid his rent or worked on the farm for months. Abigail wanted to offer this house to John's friend, but Hayden refused to move. Since Hayden lived alone, Abigail then asked if he would share the house with the refugees. Again, Hayden refused.

Abigail was furious. Many families made room for two or even three families in their small homes, yet here was a single man selfishly refusing to make room for one family. To make matters worse, Hayden told Abigail that he wouldn't take orders from her, but only from John. Finally John sent Hayden a letter ordering him to move. Only then did Hayden agree.

Although her farm was not under direct attack, Abigail faced other problems. Because so many men were needed to fight, it was hard to find people to help her with farmwork. Abigail and the children relied on the farm for many of their necessities. She would often end her letters by asking John to send her things she lacked, such as pins, sugar, or coffee. Many items that she used to buy were no longer available because of the war.

Abigail joined together with other women to weave cloth for clothing. They believed that producing their own goods instead of buying things imported from Europe was an act of patriotism. Abigail felt that this was another way she could help the cause of independence.

Women gathered together to spin flax and wool. The cloth made from this was called "homespun" or "linsey-woolsey." Making and wearing homespun clothing became the mark of a Patriot.

Faced with many hardships, Abigail kept a positive attitude that sometimes surprised even her! But then a terrible epidemic of dysentery, an intestinal problem often caused by bacteria or parasites in drinking water, struck Braintree and nearby towns. Almost everyone in the Adams house became sick, including Abigail.

Abigail recovered, but because so many other people were ill, she had to care for her family and servants while she was still weak. When her mother became ill, Abigail traveled between her home and her mother's home in order to take care of her as well. Unfortunately, her mother never recovered. Abigail was filled with grief. The fact that John was still gone made the grief even harder to bear. Abigail missed both her mother and her husband. She felt that she had sacrificed so much for her country. Though John could not help her, at least he understood the challenges she was facing. He wrote to her, "You are really brave, my dear, you are [a] heroine."

When John came home for Christmas that year, he and Abigail discussed whether he should resign as a member of Congress. Living apart had been difficult for both of them, but particularly for Abigail. She had to carry the burden of responsibility for the farm, their finances, and the children during a time of war. John left the decision up to her—should he stay on the farm or go back to Congress?

John's work in Philadelphia would be focused on the monumental task of building a new nation. Although Abigail desperately wanted him to stay home, she believed that serving the public was more important than her family's personal happiness. She told John that he should go back to Philadelphia.

Independence for All?

In the spring of 1776, Abigail Adams watched the British sail out of Boston harbor. Although the war was far from over, America was moving closer to independence from Britain. Abigail spent a lot of time thinking about the new government they would have. The issue of slavery had bothered her for a long time. She believed that it was not right that people fighting for liberty should deprive other people of their freedom.

Abigail also felt that the new government should treat women more fairly. At that time, women could not own property, attend college, or vote. In fact, under English law, men owned their wives. Yet Abigail and many other women were working, struggling, and sacrificing in the name of liberty. Why shouldn't they benefit from that liberty? Abigail felt that women should be given freedom and rights along with men, and she shared these thoughts in a letter to John.

"I desire you would Remember the Ladies… Do not put such unlimited power into the hands of the Husbands… If perticuliar care and attention is not paid to the Laidies we are determined to foment a Rebelion, and will not hold ourselves bound by any Laws in which we have no voice, or Representation."

A Adams

Abigail became one of the first Americans to speak up for women's rights. John did not agree that women should have the same freedoms as men and told her so in his reply.

Abigail was not happy with John's response. She wrote back, "I can not say that I think you very generous to the Ladies, for whilst you are proclaiming peace and good will to Men, Emancipating all Nations, you insist upon retaining an absolute power over Wives."

Abigail had spoken her mind, but beyond that she could not do much to further the cause of women's rights. She continued running the farm, paying the bills, caring for her children, and enduring the loneliness that grew more and more tedious.

Then in June, an epidemic of smallpox broke out. Abigail decided to move her family to Boston so they could be inoculated against the dreaded disease. This process was often dangerous, so Abigail did not make the decision to inoculate herself and her children lightly.

Shortly before they began the process of inoculation, Abigail and her family received groundbreaking news in a letter from John.

Smallpox Smallpox was a dangerous disease that was often fatal. In order to avoid catching a bad case, many people had themselves inoculated. This involved injecting a small amount of the smallpox virus under the skin, thereby causing a mild case of smallpox, from which most people recovered. Once exposed to smallpox, a person had to be isolated from anyone who hadn't had the disease. For this reason, whole families would often undergo inoculation together.

The Declaration

John's letter announced that the Declaration of Independence had been signed on July 4, 1776. Abigail felt happy and proud that John had been part of the important work of forming a new government. On July 18, she joined the other people of Boston in the town square to hear the public reading of the Declaration.

The crowd was silent, listening to every word. The minute the last word was spoken, everybody began cheering. Describing to John the excitement she and the others felt, Abigail wrote, "The Bells rang, the privateers fired, the forts and Batteries, the cannon were discharged, the platoons followed, and every face appeard joyfull."

It seemed to Abigail that her sacrifices, and those of other colonial women, had finally been rewarded.

The Declaration of Independence was read aloud in town squares throughout the colonies.

Afterword

The Revolutionary War continued for several more years, and so did Abigail's sacrifices for her country. She remained separated from her husband while John went first to France and then to Britain to negotiate a peace treaty. She joined him in Europe in 1784.

John Adams became the nation's second President in 1797. While she was First Lady, Abigail's interest in politics was put to use. Her opinions were well known, and she continued to express them in letters to family and friends.

Abigail was the first First Lady to live in the White House, though she and John only lived there for four months. At that time, the White House was unfinished, so Abigail had to put up with unplastered walls, no indoor plumbing, the smell of paint, and the sound of hammering. Many rooms were not ready, so Abigail hung the family's laundry in what is now the East Room!

Abigail Adams died on October 28, 1818, at the age of 73. Many years after her death, one of her grandsons published some of her letters. This became the first book written by a First Lady.

The Life of Abigail Adams

1744   Abigail Smith is born.

1764   Abigail Smith marries John Adams and becomes Abigail Adams.

1765   Abigail and John's daughter, Abigail Jr., is born.

1767   Abigail and John's son John Quincy is born.

1770   Abigail and John's son Charles is born. The Boston Massacre occurs.

1772   Abigail and John's son Thomas is born. John Adams is elected to the Massachusetts Assembly.

1773   The Boston Tea Party is held in Boston Harbor.

1774   John Adams goes to Philadelphia to attend the Continental Congress.

1775   Battles are fought at Lexington and Concord. The Battle of Bunker Hill is fought.

1776   The Declaration of Independence is signed.

1778   John Adams goes to Europe.

1783   The Revolutionary War ends.

1784   Abigail Adams goes to Europe.

1797   John Adams is elected second President of the United States.

1818   Abigail Adams dies.

Responding

 **TARGET SKILL** **Compare and Contrast** How were Abigail and John Adams's efforts and beliefs alike? How were they different?

Abigail Adams   **Both**   **John Adams**

?

believed the colonies should be free

?

Write About It

Text to Text Think about another book you have read about someone who has made important contributions to a cause. Write several paragraphs summarizing that person's contributions. Include specific examples.

efficient	peal
lacked	personally
mimic	rural
mocking	summons
organize	tedious

EXPAND YOUR VOCABULARY

assembly	legislators
congress	negotiate
emancipating	patriotism
foment	

✔ **TARGET SKILL** **Compare and Contrast** Examine how two or more details or ideas are alike and different.

✔ **TARGET STRATEGY** **Monitor/Clarify** As you read, notice what isn't making sense. Find ways to figure out the parts that are confusing.

GENRE Narrative Nonfiction gives factual information by telling a true story.